Twice Born Son

Twice Born Son

Hope for Our Walking Wounded

Ann Varley

VANTAGE PRESS
New York

Published by Vantage Press, Inc.
419 Park Ave. South, New York, NY 10016

Manufactured in the United States of America
ISBN: 978-0-533-15979-6

Library of Congress Catalog Card No: 2008900278

0 9 8 7 6 5 4 3 2 1

Contents

Author's Note

When a crisis of great proportion comes into our life, we have two choices; either we let it destroy us, or we embrace it. We don't immediately see it this way, but as time passes, we find it necessary to choose.

It is my hope and prayer that those of you who read this book, especially if you can relate to its content in any way, will be encouraged. If its words inform and make you feel less alone in your struggle, then it will have served its purpose. And for those who have been spared this journey, may you have a deeper understanding and compassion for our walking wounded.

On the morning after my son's devastating accident, eighteen years ago, I sat in the soft-pre-dawn light of a coffee shop, listening to Bette Midler singing a song from the movie, *Beaches*. The words: "You are the wind beneath my wings" repeated themselves, over and over, in my heart. They have continued to do so many times since then. For me, that Wind has been my God, who has carried me through difficult times and sustained my hope. It has also been the many people who have reached out to Jeff and me in innumerable ways. It is to them that I dedicate this book, so that they may realize the impact of their kindness.

To Tony and Diane Salpeitro, whose constant kindness sustained us during those first difficult months. Thank you.

To Father Ed Correia, Denise and Paul Lamoureux, and the churches of Freetown, for the funds and food which allowed me to be there for Jeff during that first year, thank you. To Jim and Cheryl Quirk and the girls, who have always been like family to us, thank you. To father George Harrison, for your prayers and special blessing, thank you. To Rev. Tom Monk and the many young and old, who stormed heaven with prayers for Jeff—and me—thank you.

To Denita Trembly, Mary Kinnane, Denise St. Ives, Cheryl Feeney, Lynn Amaral, Joanne Rzasa, all my dear teacher friends, and others who welcomed me to St. Stanislaus School and supported me through good times and bad, thank you.

To all those who have encouraged me to write this book, my family, especially my niece, Jackie, who typed my book for me, and my dear friends Pat Galkowski, who proofread for me, Jean and Paul Gibson, Jeannette Whipp, and Denise Medeiros, thank you.

And to Bob Varley, who made this journey in your own way, thank you for being here for us now.

You will find that almost all names of people and places in this book have been changed to protect privacy. Several others, who came to our aid in a special way, have permitted me to use their first names, one his last name, and I gratefully did so.

Our Walking Wounded

I walk like you; I talk like you,
But I am not like you.
I ask, not for your pity, but for your
Understanding.

The world, as I once knew it,
Does not exist anymore for me.
My words and my actions do not
Flow as they once did.

I question myself at every turn
And fear the judgment of my peers.

At times my differences are like a
Chain around my throat.
They choke my spontaneity and confuse
My thoughts.

I long to have my load lightened,
To fly aloft as I once did.
Please try to understand the miracle
Of my existence,

And walk with me with open minds—
For, in our hearts, we are surely the same.

—Jeff's Mom

Twice Born Son

1

Storm Clouds

Thunder rumbled in the distance. *Someone's getting a storm*, I said to myself, as I left the nursing home on that muggy July afternoon. It was my first day as the new activity director. I looked forward to putting my feet up and sipping a cold drink. Glancing again at the ominous sky, a small fear gripped me. I shook it off and concentrated on what I could pick up for supper. Jeff would be home soon.

My teenaged son had just completed his junior year at Algonquin High School. He had a part-tine job across town working with dogs twice a day. Jeff was a typical 80's kid, with long hair and a tattoo on his upper arm. Although he was capable of being a good student, he'd rather be socializing with his buddies. This summer he needed to read the final book assigned by his English teacher and pass a test on it before entering his senior year. He couldn't have cared less.

As a single mother and a schoolteacher, I frequently preached to him about the importance of school. He would either "Yes, Mom" me to death or remind me that he was NOT the All-American boy on the cereal box. I wanted so much for him but was thankful that he was such a loving child. Daily I prayed, "Lord, take care of my son!"

Every Mother's Fear

The sky darkened as I approached the house and looked for Jeff's car in the driveway. He wasn't home yet. It was just after 5:30 when I walked in the door to the jangle of the phone. "Hello?"

"This is the Freetown Police calling. Do you have a son named Jeffrey?"

Somehow, I managed a "yes."

"Your son has been in an accident," the voice continued. "He is in Grayson Memorial Hospital. We suggest that you get there as soon as possible."

"Is he badly hurt?" I gasped.

"He sustained injury, Ma'am."

"But how serious is it?"

"He sustained injury, Ma'am."

It was obvious that police protocol would not allow him to tell me more. I hung up, took several deep breaths, and called Jeff's dad. Unable to locate his father, I phoned my close friend, Cheryl. She lived across town, much nearer Grayson Memorial than we did, and she offered to take me there. Could I drive myself the six miles to her house? I took another deep breath. Time was of the essence. I must somehow find the strength to calm my racing heart and get there. And I did.

Amidst the bustle of the emergency room, I sat with my friend in a small waiting area. Was Jeff alive? Neither of us could ask this question aloud. Minutes passed, and then suddenly, a doctor appeared in the doorway.

"Mrs. Varley?" I nodded. "Your son is having a CAT Scan. You may see him when they bring him down." Some of the heaviness lifted from my chest. Jeff would be O.K. It wasn't so bad after all.

Can This Be My Son?

A nurse ushered me into a curtained cubicle. On the gurney, a figure thrashed about, groping for the numerous tubes attached by needles to his arms. An oxygen mask covered his nose and mouth. His eyes were open but unseeing. Strange sounds came from his throat.

As the nurse gently cupped my elbow and led me away, she explained, "Your son has sustained a CHI, a closed head injury. The doctor feels that he should be transported to a trauma center immediately. Hope Hospital in Boston has a bed available in its Surgical Intensive Care Unit. We had hoped to helicopter him there, but Boston is fogged in. An ambulance will take him. You may follow in a car."

Jeff's father had found my frantic message and soon arrived at Grayson Memorial. The ride to Boston was long and quiet. What were we facing if Jeff survived? If he survived? He HAD to survive! Life without our only son was unthinkable. His dad and I had been separated for four years, but our son was a strong bond between us, a joy we continued to share.

Images of closed head injured patients flooded my mind. Two years earlier I had worked briefly in a trauma unit of a long-term care facility. There I witnessed the terrible consequences of trauma on the minds and bodies of young accident victims, many of whom would never recover to lead productive lives. At that time, Jeff was taking driver education classes. I told him that every class should walk through a trauma unit as a part of the driver's ed course. Perhaps then, they would understand how speed or alcohol, often both, could shatter lives.

I never did take him to visit my unit, but to this day, my heart aches for those beautiful young people and their families. I was sure that to lose a child to death or catastrophic injury was more than I could bear, a parent's worst nightmare. Now this nightmare was mine. My heart cried out, "Lord, take care of my son!"

The Next 48 Hours

We arrived at Hope Hospital in time to see Jeff whisked past us, accompanied by a Grayson Hospital nurse, holding life-sustaining equipment. The hours ticked by with no word. Other gurneys passed, carrying knife and gunshot victims. Jeff's dad suggested that these last probably required more urgent care than Jeff, and our hopes rose. Then, just past midnight, the nurse from Grayson emerged. She placed her hand on my arm and said with obvious deep concern, "Good luck, Mother." At that moment, I knew for certain that Jeff's life hung in the balance.

Finally, at 3:30 a.m., we were taken to the Surgical Intensive Care Unit, where Jeff lay in a deep coma, mouth and nose tubes leading to his stomach and lungs, machines recording his vital signs. It had taken all these hours to stabilize him. Would he live? The next forty-eight hours would determine this. We drove back to River View as the sun rose over Boston Harbor.

2

Grim News

Day two brought an early morning call from Dr. Griffin, the neurosurgeon in charge of Jeffrey's case at Hope Hospital. He explained the need to insert a cranial bolt into Jeff's head to measure brain pressure. Severe swelling of the brain had put him at great risk. This must be constantly monitored in order to control it with appropriate amounts of medication.

The bolt would touch Jeff's brain and extend several inches beyond his skull. A cone-shaped bandage would surround it to help prevent infection. My permission was necessary. Hard as it was to envision this procedure, I agreed, certain that he was in competent hands.

As I entered Jeff's room several hours later, I tried to prepare for what I might see. Was this truly my son? His long hair had been roughly cut, and one side shaved to accommodate the cranial bolt. More tubes protruded from his body. His legs were fitted with tube-like stockings, which expanded rhythmically to aid circulation and prevent an embolism.

Periodically, his nurse came to check the readings on the machines. Each time they carefully examined his eyes, holding them wide open with their fingers, making sure that his brain function had not stopped, even as the machine kept his body alive.

The Care of Many Hands

On this day I learned that Jeff was being cared for by a team of doctors, headed by the neurosurgeon. They met daily, more often, if necessary, to discuss his progress and treatment. Forty-eight hours after the accident, I was taken aside and told that Jeff's condition was still termed "grim." The latest CAT scan revealed additional cranial bleeding. When brain cells are inundated by blood, shutting off the oxygen supply, they die and are sloughed off. This occurs when the injured brain swells and presses against the skull. In desperation, I asked if his skull couldn't be opened to relieve this pressure. Sadly, this was not a possibility with CHI, a closed head injury, like Jeff's. Perhaps, future medical advances would make such surgery available, but not in time for Jeff.

To further complicate his condition, Jeff's right lung had collapsed. Surgery was necessary to insert a tube and inflate it. Clearly, my son, although still alive, had not made the progress hoped for during these initial forty-eight hours. To the contrary, his response to the life-saving procedures ordered by his doctors had been minimal.

Into the Lord's Hands

When I gave my permission for doctors to inflate Jeff's collapsed lung, his medical team proposed a last-resort treatment. He would be placed in a chemically induced coma, in addition to his own injury-induced coma. This would slow his life functions to the minimum, decreasing the flow of blood that surged to his brain every time his heart beat. Hopefully, this would cause the swelling to decrease. It was risky, but necessary, if Jeff were to survive. A monitor would be placed in his heart. Should it stop beating, this device would alert his caregivers, who would then attempt to revive him. The chemical used to induce this type of coma becomes toxic to the body after forty-eight hours. Should Jeff not respond to this final treatment within ten to fifteen hours, there was little hope that he ever would. Their records attested to this.

The staff suggested that we remain close by. Family quarters at Hope Hospital's SICU were being renovated, so my niece and I spent the night in the unit's waiting room, sleeping fitfully on a cramped couch and the floor. I was so close to my son, but so far from being able to help him—except by prayer. I thought of Christ's plea to his father in the garden, "Father, let this cup pass from me."

"Lord, let my child live!" I prayed. Then I remembered the conclusion of this prayer of Christ, "Not my will, Father, but yours be done." Now I needed to embrace His will.

At some point during that long night, a nurse came to tell us that Jeff had survived the latest procedures. For almost another forty-eight hours we would wait—and pray.

Friday, day four dawned, and with the morning came the realization that thirty-six hours had passed with no response to the chemically induced coma. Twelve hours remained before Jeff would be lightened from his coma, to avoid toxicity. What then?

"Your Will Be Done, Father."

The Sacrament of the Sick

Mid-morning, Father Harrison arrived to administer the Sacrament of the Sick, which Catholics receive in case of serious illness or imminent death. I stood at the foot of Jeff's bed, feeling somehow disconnected from my body, a spectator looking on from a distance. After the final anointing, Father placed his hands on Jeff's head, the cranial bolt protruding between his fingers, and prayed, "Jesus, you know Jeffrey. You know his goodness. YOU CAN HEAL THIS HEAD!"

I spent the rest of the day sitting by my son's side, silent tears slipping slowly down my cheeks. Jeff's caregivers came and went, the machines made their usual beeps. Nothing changed, nothing except my heart. Gradually, a deep peace replaced the anxiety. He was in God's hands. This was my Good Friday. I gave Jeff back to the Father.

"How will he die?" I asked the doctor, who held my hands and told me that Jeff was not responding, that there was nothing more they could do. Gently, she explained, "As his brain swells, it will exert pressure on the brain stem, located at the base of the skull. This pressure will cut off impulses to heart and lungs. He'll feel no pain. You can go home now. We'll call you if we need you."

3

Hope Renewed

During these first critical days, my sleep consisted of four or five hours nightly. The blackness that enveloped my mind was totally devoid of the stark reality I was facing. I awakened quickly from these periods of merciful oblivion as if touched by a live wire. Reality returned!

The clock showed Saturday, 4:30 a.m. My thoughts raced back to the conversation of the previous evening. No call! Jeff had survived the night. Years before, I had read a book titled *And with the Dawn Rejoicing,* a verse taken from the Book of Psalms in the Old Testament. Dared I hope?

Parents were encouraged to call Hope Hospital's ICU at any time, yet I hesitated, fearful that this slender thread of hope might be severed. I made the call as the first rays of summer sun touched my windows. Jeff's nurse was busy with him, I was told. She would take my call as soon as possible. Minutes ticked by. "Your will be done, Father."

Then, as my room filled with sunlight, I heard the words, "Jeff stabilized during the night. His intracranial brain pressure has returned to normal. We've begun to lighten him from his chemically induced coma."

Later, I was told that he had fought constantly to overcome that induced coma. This had made it necessary to administer many doses of medication. His young body was putting up a valiant battle for life!

The Fight Continues

But, the battle wasn't over. Hours after his arrival at the hospital, Jeff's right side had begun to show signs of posturing. His arms and legs began to contract in a grotesque manner. This was a strong indication that paralysis was affecting these areas. By the end of week one, Jeff's right side was paralyzed. Difficult as it was to imagine his life in a wheelchair, the hope that he would survive his terrible trauma made all things seem acceptable. We would face life together.

During the following week, the highs and lows continued. As his brain pressure normalized, his body temperature rose, each day slightly higher than the last. This caused great concern. Was there infection that a CAT scan failed to pick up? Were his tubes carrying bacteria to the lungs or other areas of the body? Surgery is usually not done when high fever is present, but Jeff's doctors had no other option. Again, I trusted their judgment. They performed a tracheotomy, the insertion of a tube through an incision in the throat. This greatly reduces the danger of respiratory infection and continues to assist breathing.

Next, a gastric tube was inserted in Jeff's abdomen, allowing nourishment and medication to enter his stomach directly. Lastly, an exploratory incision was made in an attempt to locate any source of infection. Nothing was found. During surgery, Jeff's right lung collapsed a second time since the accident, and was again successfully inflated. As I was reminded by one of his nurses, he had youth on his side—youth and the prayers of so many good people.

A Time to Live/A Time to Die

On Sunday, day six, several of my friends from the Sisters of St. Joseph visited. They looked at my son and softly began prayers for a happy death. As I gazed at Jeff's face, I saw his eyes move slightly under closed lids. I KNEW he was hearing their prayers and was saying, in the only way he could, "Not yet, Mom. It's not my time to go yet."

One week after the accident, I arrived early at the hospital. Jeff's rising temperature remained of prime concern. When his neurosurgeon came by to check the chart, I asked, "Will he live, Doctor?" We walked over to my seventeen-year-old son, who had been placed on a recliner beside his bed. His right side remained paralyzed, tubes continued to help sustain life, and his eyes, although open slightly, showed no movement or recognition. After a long pause, Dr. Griffin responded, "Barring serious infection, which we can't control, I think we can say that, clinically, he will survive, but he may never be more responsive than he is now."

With a certitude that surprised even me, I announced, "If he lives, Doctor, he WILL have a quality of life!" Patiently, Dr. Griffin reminded me of the severity of Jeff's injury. He would never be the person I had known before. "But he WILL have a quality of life." I repeated. "I know this as surely as I am standing here with you!" Realizing that a mother's HOPE is all she has at a moment like this, the doctor quietly replied, "Mother, you keep right on believing this."

This was Jeff's last day in SICU, where he had been treated with such tender care. I will never forget them.

4

Progressive Care

In the Progressive Care Unit, Jeff was placed in a room where he could be constantly observed by the nurses. Soaring temperatures and violent tremors further threatened his life. Sweat drops of giant proportion poured off his body; the infection Dr. Griffin had mentioned, one that couldn't be controlled. Culture after culture failed to reveal the cause. Hope hung in the balance. Finally, after five long days, the lab had success, and with appropriate treatment, a slow but steady improvement was evident. Now, we could concentrate on recovery.

Jeff was soon moved out of direct view of the nurses' station, but they continued to look for signs of consciousness. I was learning that, contrary to many hospital scenes viewed on T.V. and movie screens, awakening from a coma is a slow process. Some patients remain in a constant vegetative state, unaware of anything around them. They require twenty-four hour care and usually spend their lives in a long-term care facility. If Jeff remained in his present state, this might well be his future. My mind refused to go there. Other patients progress to varying levels of recognition and understanding. There are many ways used by caregivers to foster this return to consciousness.

When caring for him, Jeff's nurses talked to him continually. Family and friends were urged to do the same, recalling familiar people and events. His buddies came and told him jokes. They teased him about his "great" hair-do and his numerous tubes. We brought his favorite after shave and cologne, always hoping that a familiar voice or odor would trigger some response. NOTHING!

I was taught to exercise Jeff's legs daily. Since his arrival at Hope Hospital, he had been dressed in socks and his own sneakers to prevent foot drop, a muscle weakness, which would impede his walking if and when he recovered. His eyes were open slightly wider now, but they remained dull and empty. He was in his own distant world.

A Mother's Voice

When I read to him, I sat on Jeff's right side. His paralysis caused him to turn his head in that direction. Since content wasn't important, I chose random sections from the *Reader's Digest.* After each paragraph or two, I looked up at my son, always hoping to see a flicker of recognition or the hint of a smile.

On this particular day, the article I was reading caught my interest. I read continually for about ten minutes. The story over, I looked up at Jeff. His eyes, wide open and glistening, gazed steadily into mine. "Well, HELLO there!" I said in a voice chocked with tears. As I rushed to the left side of the bed, Jeff's head turned with my movements, his eyes never leaving mine. I sat down, this time on his "good" side, and took his hand. "Jeff, you've had a bad accident, but you WILL get better. You know I've never lied to you. If you believe me, squeeze my hand." Very slowly, Jeff's fingers tightened around mine. HE SQUEEZED MY HAND!

Mountains to Move

After a week in Progressive Care, the idea of rehabilitation was mentioned to me. Several people had noticed slight movement in Jeff's right leg, and he was responding to simple verbal commands. His "balloon" trach prevented any oral response, but he definitely understood what people said.

I visited two rehabilitation facilities that were suggested to me. Both had much to offer, but I chose Maplewood. There, they encouraged family involvement with the patient from day one. It proved to be an excellent choice. However, this move was not without its angst.

Maplewood was known as a rapid rehabilitation facility, with a quick patient turnover. Not everyone qualified to go there. A Maplewood nurse was sent to Hope Hospital to evaluate Jeff's present condition. She greeted me cheerfully at the nurses' station and sent me for coffee while she examined him. When I returned, her manner was solemn. She explained that Jeff had made far less progress than she anticipated. Maplewood would accept him as a patient and bring him along as far as possible. However, I needed to understand that he might require long-term care.

Once again, I stormed Heaven, reminding God that Scripture assures us that faith will move mountains. I prayed, "Lord, move this mountain!"

5

Rehabilitation

On August 4, Jeff was transported by ambulance to Maplewood Rehabilitation Facility, having been at Hope Hospital for almost four weeks. I was not able to ride in the ambulance with him. I doubt if there would have been room, with Jeff's gurney, his various machines, and the attending nurse.

When I arrived, he was settled in a double occupancy room. I talked to the head nurse, Lynn. She had taken an immediate interest in Jeff, this boy who was wheeled in, as she would later describe to me, hooked up with three tubes, no movement in his right side, nothing verbal; just those eyes tracking her. Would they be able to help this poor kid here at Maplewood, she wondered?

A Ray of Hope

But, Jeff was in the right place. Four days later, a Monday, the head physical therapist, who was seeing him for the first time, read the evaluations at the nurses' station. She then examined Jeff herself. She couldn't believe her findings! Yes, he still had tubes and a trach, but he seemed greatly improved. She greeted me with this good news when I arrived for the four p.m. visiting hours. The mountain was moving!

About ten days after Jeff's admission to Maplewood, I was shocked to find him restrained in his bed. A vest tied to the head rail kept his torso from any quick movements. Each hand was mitted and fastened to the side bed rail. He appeared agitated, almost angry. What was this sudden change? Within a few minutes, Jeff's male nurse appeared and quickly took me to a nearby porch to explain what was happening. "As your son gradually emerges from his coma," he said, "the body, in all its parts, is awakening, causing this agitation. It's a VERY necessary stage in his recovery, but extremely difficult to watch. If he doesn't experience it, he won't continue to move forward. In some instances, a patient will remain in this stage, but the majority move beyond it. This is what we hope for Jeff."

For several days, Jeff's bed was wheeled to the nurses' station in order to monitor him, especially at night. He had already managed to free one hand in an attempt to get out of bed. Then, gradually, the struggling subsided. Soon, I was greeted with a smile from my restraint-free son. He had turned another corner.

Beginning with Small Steps

Being a rapid rehab facility, Maplewood was bustling with myriad activities from early morning until 4 p.m. Only then were visitors welcome. There was one exception. One day a week, a close relative was urged to come and sit in on the day's activities. In this way, he or she could measure the progress of a loved one from week to week. My day was Wednesday. The first activity I observed was speech therapy. I was devastated!

Jeff was in his wheelchair with the therapist seated in front of him. He was turning his head from side to side, oblivious to everyone in the room. I sat at a distance, but could easily observe. The session went as follows:

Therapist: "Is your name Jeff Varley? Nod 'yes' or 'no.' "
Jeff: No nod. Head still moving from side to side.

16

Therapist: Repeats question. (Gently moves Jeff's face toward her.) Repeats question.

Jeff: Nods "yes."

This went on, using other questions, such as: "Did you have an accident? Are you seventeen? Are you in the hospital?" Always, the therapist had to turn Jeff's face toward her to gain his attention. I was stunned when she announced that this first session had gone "very well." I fought back the tears.

The next Wednesday, I almost dreaded another speech session, but to my amazement, Jeff answered each question with an immediate correct nod or gesture. The mountain was STILL moving!

The following week, I observed Jeff at physical therapy. Two attendants lifted him from his wheelchair, each holding him firmly. His right leg now had sufficient movement, but neither leg seemed able to take a step forward without criss-crossing the other. At this point each therapist lifted one of Jeff's legs, first the right, then the left, with her own foot, in a walking pattern. After five or six such steps, he slumped forward, completely exhausted. He was then placed on a large raised mat, but refused to exercise further. Jeff's therapist explained that a serious head injury creates so many traumas throughout the body, and recovery requires so much energy, that the patient is constantly exhausted in the initial phases of therapy.

A week later, I sat in on occupational therapy. Here, the patient works on activities that improve the body's fine motor skills above the waist. Jeff was seated in front of a table game called "Battleship." Instead of striving to beat an opponent, he was asked to place a peg in a given hole on the game board. Simply picking UP one of the pegs presented a big challenge for him. Placing it IN a specific hole took five or six attempts and caused much frustration. He let his therapist know he wasn't happy, but I could see him struggle for control. She was young and cute. Jeff hadn't lost his eye for a pretty girl. Praise God!

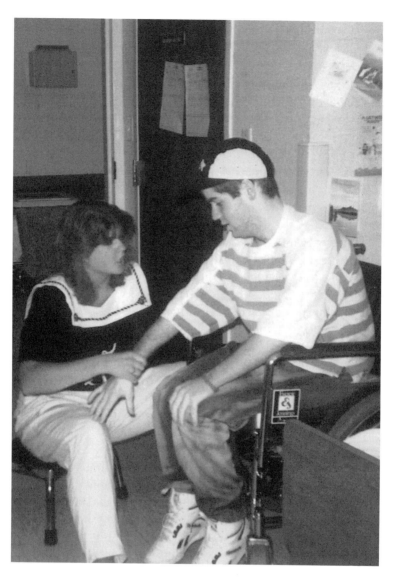

Jeff during an occupational therapy session at Maplewood Rehab.

Although he lacked the dexterity of former days, when he enjoyed playing the guitar, some movement had returned to Jeff's right arm and hand. I noticed that he was using his left hand for things requiring strength, but being a natural right-hander, never depended on it completely. Gradually, like a kindergartener learning to print his name, he was able to write quite legibly.

As Jeff's rehab continued, it became apparent that he was beginning to beat the odds. This "poor kid" was making daily progress, and people were beginning to notice, especially Lynn, Jeff's favorite nurse. She accompanied Dr. Greene, the administrator of Maplewood, on his frequent trips through the wards. Each time he looked at Jeff and reviewed his chart, he would say, "I didn't see this happening." Things were looking hopeful.

Large and Small Victories

Jeff's serious balance problem was addressed next. Fortunately, Maplewood had recently purchased a computer-based machine, the first of its kind, which deals with issues of balance. Jeff was the first to use it. After being securely fastened to avoid a fall from the machine, he could maneuver his body back and forth and from side to side, as he attempted, while in a standing position, to match his movements with markers on a computer screen positioned in front of him. The results were remarkable! Were it not for this marvelous piece of equipment, Jeff's ability to walk normally again might have remained severely compromised.

As the weeks passed, Jeff's balloon trach, which had not allowed any speaking, was removed. It was replaced by a simpler device that made it possible to talk, if only in a whisper. Imagine my joy, when I entered his room to find him sitting in his wheelchair and was greeted by the husky words, "Hi, Mom!" His words never sounded so sweet.

Soon after that, he met me coming down the hall to the

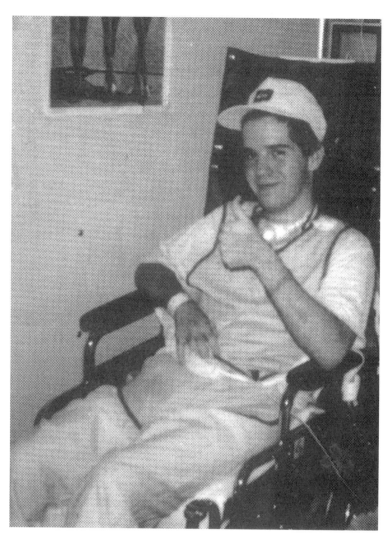

Jeff at Maplewood giving me a thumbs-up and greeting me with a husky, "Hi, Mom!"

nurses' station, handling a walker completely on his own; his therapists close by on either side. The wide smile on his face seemed to say, "Look, Mom, I'm WALKING!"

Back at Hope Hospital, weeks before, Dr. Griffin had reminded me that if Jeff did survive, I would not have the same son as before. At that time, my mind had refused to accept that possibility. I could only think, *Just let him live and with a mother's love and care he will heal.*

A Long Road Ahead

Now, almost seven weeks later, having witnessed so many medical procedures and been counseled so wisely by his caregivers, I realized that Jeff's journey through life would be quite different from what I had envisioned. Yet, there WAS still hope—hope for that certain quality of life that I had foreseen weeks before, when he lay in a deep coma. Somehow, I would deal with his deficits, sure in the knowledge that the Jeff I knew was still there. It would require much effort and more tears, but with faith and hope, small miracles do happen.

One of the most difficult aspects of post-traumatic behavior is anger and frustration. Some patients need to relearn the rules of social courtesy, evidenced by inappropriate remarks, sometimes sexual in content, when in a social setting. I was advised that almost always, a patient's most negative pre-trauma behavior trait was the one that would dominate his post-traumatic life. This proved to be true in Jeff's case. His "short fuse" had always been a challenge. It was genetic, as well as post-trauma. We would both need much patience in the future to deal with this.

6

Homeward Bound

In early September, Jeff had minor surgery to remove granulated tissue around his tracheotomy. In a surprise move, the doctor decided to have him spend the night without his trach, while his breathing was closely monitored. He did very well. Still, there was serious concern that his throat muscles had been weakened by his paralysis. This could make it necessary for him to eat pureed food, at least initially, once his trach and stomach tubes were no longer necessary.

Again, the wonders of modern technology came to Jeff's aid. Now that the trach was soon to be removed, his swallowing ability could be tested on another of Maplewood's new machines. It would show a food particle as it passed through the esophagus, guided by the rhythmical working of a series of throat muscles. The rhythm must be perfect to avoid choking or aspirating material into the lungs, causing serious problems.

I was not expecting this test to be done until the following day, nor did I know that the trach had been permanently removed. Shortly after twelve noon the day following Jeff's surgery, a phone call brought this announcement from a very delighted seventeen-year-old, "Mom, I just had a cheeseburger for lunch!" I didn't believe him. I could hear the laughter in the background, as Jeff assured me that it was true. "Here, I'll let you speak to a nurse," he said. It was indeed true. He had passed the swallowing test that morning, with no problems. No pureed food for him!

When the nurses asked him what he wanted for lunch to celebrate, he had said a cheeseburger, and that is just what they got him. My heart rejoiced. I was getting my son back!

Once Jeff was tube-free and eating normally, he was permitted to leave Maplewood on day trips. The first was to a nearby restaurant, accompanied by his parents and his girlfriend. It was encouraging to know that no staff member was considered necessary. He used a walker with front wheels. Negotiating corners and small spaces required some help, but overall, it was a very successful trip. Soon, Jeff progressed to Sundays at home and a reunion with his beloved cats. Friends came over, but conversation was a bit awkward. The easy comradeships were missing. They seemed to be silently asking, "Where is the Jeff we knew?"

Back at Maplewood, he continued his therapies, climbing up and down a short flight of portable stairs and practicing getting in and out of a car. I wheeled him to the cafeteria each night for supper. His right hand, with its fine motor skills compromised, made some actions difficult. Cutting food, spreading butter on bread, and picking up small pieces of food with a fork tried Jeff's patience. Several times he threatened to dump his plate on the floor, and his language was not the best. People there seldom noticed. They were struggling with their own problems or those of loved ones. A breakthrough came one evening when he looked at me and said, "Mom, I guess I'd better get my act together." A few days later, I would better understand the full meaning of Jeff's words in the cafeteria.

Unwelcome News

I was being driven to Hope Hospital by my teacher friend, Beverly Hogan, who had recently become aware of facts she wanted to share with me. Quietly, she told me that on the day of Jeff's accident, he and two of his friends had been drinking. One of these friends had purchased the liquor, and Jeff had lacked the good sense to say "no." When his friends realized the consequences of their drinking, they were deeply upset, and one confided in Mrs. Hogan. Now I knew why they had called so often to check on Jeff, and how relieved they were as he improved.

I was in denial at first, but gradually began to accept the sad truth. How skillfully Jeff had managed to hide his drinking from me. Every night when he arrived home, he would come in and kiss me goodnight. I never detected liquor on his breath. Perhaps it was better that I hadn't known until now. My plate had been full enough. It was another hurdle that we would have to address when Jeff came home. And what a hurdle it would be!

Teenage Angst

October 6th was set as the tentative discharge date. As it approached, Jeff grew increasingly frustrated with hospital restrictions. He still was required to use a wheelchair to go out to the porch. One day, as we passed the nurses' station on the way out, a nurse standing nearby looked up and greeted him. She had watched him, step by step, beat the odds. But this was obviously not one of Jeff's best days. The interchange went something like this:

"Hi, Jeff, how are ya doin'?"

"I want to get out of this hell hole!"

The nurse, seeming not at all surprised by his response, placed his frowning face between her two hands and chirped cheerfully. "Where's our sweet little Jeff?" Then, before he could answer, she stepped back and continued, "Good for you, Jeff! That's EXACTLY what we want to hear! We want you out of here, too."

Goodbye, Maplewood

This appeared to be a turning point. Within days, we were given the welcome news that Jeff would be discharged on September 29th, a week earlier than previously planned. He was ready. Dr. Greene met with Jeff's father and me shortly before his discharge. He showed us the latest CAT scan of Jeff's skull. The upper left frontal lobe and the lower right back lobe showed substantial cell damage. Less was evident throughout the remaining areas. As I looked at that dear damaged skull, I wondered what future there could be for my seventeen-year-old son, my only child. Then I remembered the mountain God had already moved.

When leaving Maplewood, there were many instructions regarding Jeff's still impaired balance. He was urged to bring home a cane, but he'd have no part of that. Exercises at home and at a local rehabilitation center were a must. Physical, occupational, and speech therapy twice a week would continue. We were to return to Maplewood for monthly evaluations.

I will be forever grateful to the dedicated people at Maplewood. They were "the wind beneath my wings" for weeks, and would continue to be for months to come. Soon, I would begin to understand their parting words, "Good luck, Mother. Now the honeymoon is over."

7

What Honeymoon?

Certainly, the good people at Maplewood didn't think that ANYTHING during the past three months had resembled a honeymoon. Just what did their parting words mean—the honeymoon is over? It wouldn't takes me long to find out.

I'd like to say that Jeff settled into his former routines without any serious problems. That would have been unrealistic. We had both relied heavily on the personnel at Maplewood and the busy schedules that occupied so much of the day. This was a support we no longer had. What do we do now?

Difficult Moments

Jeff's lack of balance and his right side clumsiness affected everything he tried to do. It was essential that he not fall and re-injure that fragile brain. He could no longer play his guitar. The sketching of his favorite musicians or late model cars just didn't produce the same results. Reading with eyes that no longer focused well together exhausted him in minutes. Each morning we struggled through his exercises, done on a floor mat. I was his mother, insisting on these actions his body so resisted, not the therapists at Maplewood. He fought me daily, often refusing to complete them. He knew the right buttons to push. Now, it was my turn to be frustrated.

The twice-weekly therapy sessions at a nearby Maplewood satellite produced the same negative reactions in Jeff. His frequent response when I reminded him that it was time to go was, "Get out of my face! I'm O.K. the way I am!" But, he wasn't. I knew this and so did he. It hadn't taken me long to realize that the honeymoon was indeed over.

Thank You, God

And just what had been this HONEYMOON during those eight weeks at Maplewood? A little reflection told me. It was that first precious moment when I realized that my child was not going to die. It was those weekly improvements I noted at his therapy sessions, and the day he said, "Hi, Mom," for the first time. Most of all, it was the hope that sustained me through a mother's worst nightmare. I thanked God for the honeymoon. I knew that if I were to continue to be a support for Jeff, I must hold tightly to that God-given hope, no matter how bleak things might often appear.

On our October return to Maplewood, Dr. Greene encouraged Jeff to use self-control to handle his anger. Not any easy task! After our rough start at home, we had established a fairly acceptable routine. I was trying to use various "tough love" methods learned during my past rehab experience. Certain words and attitudes were NOT acceptable, and I made this very clear. We would continue our activities when HE told me he was ready. As a child, Jeff had always wanted to please. Now, given time to reflect on his words or actions, he was able to gain control of himself. An "I'm sorry," or "I love you," came in a relatively short time.

Jeff's friends stopped by occasionally. There was still that lack of easy communication, noticed previously on his home visits. A young neighbor, urged by his mother, came to play the game "Pick-Up-Sticks," one of the activities I had bought to improve

Jeff's fine motor skills. Midway through the game, Jeff knocked the remaining sticks across the table. This friend never came back.

A Broken Heart

Since his return home, Jeff and his girlfriend had talked frequently on the phone, but two weeks had passed without a visit. This was not uppermost in MY thoughts, but as I look back, I'm sure it was the ONLY thing on Jeff's mind.

One evening, having forgotten an important item on my shopping list, I decided to leave Jeff alone while I drove to a local convenience store. I poked my head into the living room and told him I'd be right back. There was no response. Jeff lay on the couch, his face turned toward the wall. Instantly, I knew something was very wrong. In a choked voice, he told me that Karen was no longer his girlfriend. He wished he were dead. I tried to be casual, as I said I would do my errand the next day. It broke my heart when he responded, "You can go to the store, Mom. Don't worry, I won't kill myself. I know what that would do to you." I went, not without fear, relieved when I returned to find him watching T.V.

Back to School

When Jeff returned home, I arranged with his teacher at Algonquin to have me work with him as he completed his summer assignment from his junior year. Since I was a certified teacher, it was quickly arranged. Jeff and I took turns reading. His double vision kicked in when he read for more than fifteen or twenty minutes at one time. After I read, I would question him on the content. His understanding and ability to express himself amazed me. It was soon evident that Jeff retained much more of what he heard than what he read. Because of this, I was allowed to give him his short quizzes orally and write down his answers. By the end of October, he was ready for the final test, using this same oral method. He passed it with flying colors. Within a week, he announced, to my delight, that he wanted to go back to school. In this instance, I could say without sadness, that this was NOT the son I had known before his injury.

Algonquin High worked with me to set up a program for Jeff. Testing revealed that his language arts skills were intact for his age and grade. His math skills, however, were a different story. The trauma had reduced them to a third grade level. Fortunately, he needed only two more credits, one in English, and the other in math, to qualify for graduation. English could be taken in a regular classroom, at a twelfth grade level, but he would require special needs instruction for math.

I was to drop Jeff off at school each morning, shortly after class started. A town vehicle would bring him home several hours later. This worked out well for me, giving me time for shopping and personal business while he was at school.

Shortly after Jeff's eighteenth birthday on November 11, he started school. He put on a good front, but I knew he was nervous. It was necessary for him to walk to and from class when no students were present in the halls. The administrators feared that although Jeff's balance was improved, he was still at risk of falling as classmates hurried by him. He shared very little school news with me but seemed to be adjusting well. Perhaps his new glasses, which greatly relieved his double vision, were making things easier.

An Emergency Call

I wasn't prepared for the call that came from Algonquin High a few weeks later. "We need you here as soon as possible," urged the guidance counselor. *Seizures*, I thought, *he's had a grand mal seizure!* On our last check up at Maplewood, Dr. Greene had taken my son off Dilantin at Jeff's request. The doctor had cautioned that stopping this seizure medication might make him more vulnerable to seizures in the future. Jeff, tired of the lethargy caused by this medicine, opted to stop. I agreed, hoping against hope that he would remain seizure-free.

"Is it a seizure? I asked as I followed Mrs. Devlin into the building. "No," she said, "he's drunk, very drunk. He's in the nurse's room. We're trying to calm him down. He's very agitated."

How could this be? I had dropped him off earlier that morning and he seemed just fine. A very unsteady Jeff greeted me with slurred complaints that everyone was picking on him; he wasn't drunk! I was able to convince him that he was, indeed, very drunk. It took two of us to get him to the car so I could drive him home. I knew that Jeff and I needed to have a serious talk, but at that moment he wanted to do nothing but sleep.

The following day we did talk. He was filled with shame and remorse. I knew he was not simply saying what he thought I wanted to hear. I saw the sadness in his eyes. Who was he? Where did he fit in? Did he have a future? Those questions were just too hard to face. He knew what would take the edge off his pain.

As mothers, we don't like to think that our children know where to get alcohol. But they do. Jeff got his and took it just before he got in the car. I thought he was cleaning his teeth at the last minute. Little did I know that he was drinking the "hard stuff" that had no odor. By the time he settled into his English class, he was feeling no pain and was escorted to the school nurse.

The Compromise

Just last spring Jeff and several classmates were found with small bottles of alcohol on their person. No one drank. It appeared to be a game of "I dare you to bring it." This went on Jeff's record as a first alcohol offense. I don't remember even being officially informed. No doubt, Jeff mentioned it to me. He found it almost impossible not to confess his misdemeanors.

As a result of this second offense, which was certainly not minor, I received another call, one telling me that Jeff, who was now a two-time offender, was being suspended for two weeks. The mother lion in me rose up to do battle. Two weeks? This boy who was tottering on the brink of serious depression! A seventeen-year-old who had been snatched from the jaws of death only four months earlier! What were they thinking! I called Maplewood and spoke with Jeff's neuropsychiatrist, a wonderful, caring woman. She gave me the information I needed. A meeting was immediately setup with Algonquin's administrators, Jeff's teacher, his guidance counselor, the school nurse, and his mother. I felt somehow empowered to do this for my son.

I was read the regulations pertaining to alcohol offenses at Algonquin. To not enforce these rules would give the appearance of favoritism and might cause resentment in students who had been suspended in the past, I was told. But, I countered, Jeff was NOT the same boy who had been found with alcohol last spring. This was the Jeff who had sustained a severe head trauma, the boy who had been somehow reborn. His ability to make sound judgments had been compromised, and this MUST be considered. Certainly, as educators, they understood this. Jeff had asked for help, not a suspension that would only further depress him. We were meeting on a Wednesday. The unanimous decision was that Jeff would return to school the following Monday. I said my silent thanks to Maplewood Rehab.

8

Graduation and Beyond

School continued to be a healthy challenge for Jeff. The fact that he could achieve in language arts gave him a feeling of normality. Math had never come easy for him. I told him this was a family trait, on his mother's side.

In late February 1990, we made our final evaluation trip to Maplewood. Dr. Greene was so pleased with Jeff's progress that he canceled his next two monthly visits. The topic of driving, the passion of every eighteen-year-old male, came up at this time. Inwardly, I shuddered at the mere thought of it. The doctor suggested that Jeff wait until late spring before giving it serious thought, although he was not adverse to the idea. He felt more time was necessary to assure us all that Jeff was ready, both mentally and physically. We were to contact him for the letter required by the Registry of Motor Vehicles when Jeff was beginning his driving lessons. To Jeff, spring was a long way off; for me, it would come much too soon.

I Got It, Mom!

June did come, and with it the joy of Jeff's graduation. He had a difficult time with his balance as he marched, with measured step, down the aisle in his cap and gown to celebrate awards day. But he managed. I thought of that other walk down the hall at

Maplewood, when he used his walker unassisted for the first time. How far he had come!

The actual presentation of diplomas took place outside a few days later. Jeff staggered a bit on the uneven ground as he hurried to receive this symbol of achievement. Then, looking for me in the crowd, he raised his right hand holding his diploma and yelled, "I got it, Mom!" People near me smiled at his enthusiasm. They had no idea of the pride I felt.

A Test Passed

Shortly before graduation, Jeff had begun classes to prepare for the driver competency test. We had a difficult time finding an instructor willing to take him on. A friend referred us to Nancy, who had experience with head injured drivers. The registry required letter from Dr. Greene arrived. There were several regulations, including one saying that Jeff must drive an automatic. The co-ordination needed for a standard might prove too difficult for him. Jeff was disappointed. A standard had always been his favorite.

He was taking to driving again, like a duck to water. After just three lessons, Jeff was ready to take the test. Imagine his surprise, when he recognized the testing officer as the same one who had failed him two years before. At the completion of that test, Jeff had pulled over, as instructed, but left the car running, a courtesy to the next student to be tested. The officer had told him, "You failed. You had a perfect test, but you didn't turn off the ignition, so you failed." There he stood in front of Jeff. After his initial shock, Jeff told himself, *I WILL pass this test*! He had no trouble doing just that.

I rejoiced that he had passed his driver's test. The look on his face when he arrived home with the news was a joy to behold. At the same time, I knew I would dread every phone call that came

"Mom, I got it!" Jeff at his graduation from Algonquin High School.

when he wasn't home and listen for the crunch of stones in our driveway, well after twelve, on many a night. Jeff's dad found an inexpensive car to get him on the road again. When it died, we replaced it with another inexpensive one. I had serious discussions with Jeff about his responsibility as a driver. Each time, he would assure me that he had learned his lesson the hard way; he would NEVER drink and drive again. I so wanted to believe him.

Driving gave Jeff more options when looking for work. After several unsuccessful interviews, he was hired as a night watchman at a box factory. It was part-time and seemed to suit him well. He had also begun dating a young girl from a nearby town. I had taught her older sister in school. By early summer, all appeared to be falling into place.

Déjà vu

It was almost midnight, when the phone rang. I tensed, as I said hello. An unfamiliar male voice asked, "Do you have a son named Jeff?" My throat constricted. I tried to say "yes," but could only manage a whisper. The man continued. "He's at my house, standing outside my window. I chose not to let him in. He's O.K., but his car went off the road and he wants you to pick him up." I knew the location. My body was still trembling as Jeff got in the car. He smelled of alcohol. This marked the beginning of what I soon called The Summer from Hell.

The next morning Jeff's car was towed to a local auto repair shop. The tire and hubcap were replaced. This would happen again in the following weeks, at no small cost. How do I explain the frustration I felt? It was the '90's, as my son so often reminded me, the decade of drink and drugs, fast cars, and few restrictions. People would look at Jeff and say to me, "Aren't you glad this is all behind you?" They hadn't a clue! In many ways, it was just beginning.

Except for his tracheotomy scar, which was red for several years, Jeff did look like the all-American boy. The difference lay within that fragile skull. Trauma had left him so vulnerable. Yes, he had the physical ability to drive, but did he have the mental dexterity to not be a risk to himself and others? The doctors trusted that he did. He knew right from wrong but could he make judgments based on assessing the future correctly, this good young man, whose ability to see anything but the "now" had been compromised?

At times I felt overwhelmed, especially when a call came from the police station in mid-August. Jeff and a girl, both underage, were found in a parked car with beer cans. A homeowner had called to report cans being thrown on his lawn. Jeff had been taken to the station, where he could only be signed out by a constable at my request. He was very drunk and verbally abusive. I was able to bring him home later that evening. As I looked up at the dark sky, I implored God to light my way.

Straight with Crooked Lines

The light came in an unexpected manner. Jeff had his first *grand mal* seizure. It was Sunday, August 25, and he was at a friend's house, several miles away. A call came from a young girl who sounded frightened. Her mother had asked her to phone me. While Jeff visited with her brother, he suddenly had fallen to the floor and couldn't stop shaking.

Luckily, the mother was a nurse and had called the paramedics. I arrived just as they were loading Jeff into the ambulance. At the hospital he was conscious and on a gurney, being questioned by a nurse. He had definitely had a *grand mal* seizure. With this type of seizure, muscles contract, causing rapid body movements, irregular breathing, and loss of consciousness.

I was advised to have Jeff rest for the remainder of the day and tomorrow, to contact a neurologist for an appointment. There would be no more driving for at least six months. Jeff's fast world had come to a screeching halt. Good! We needed time to take some deep breaths and plan for the future. Truly, God does write straight with crooked lines. Thank you, Father! Hope lives.

9

Life with Seizures

The medical term for the episode Jeff had experienced is post-traumatic epilepsy. Just the mention of the word epilepsy is frightening to most of us. It is also frightening to watch a *grand mal* seizure. The person awakens feeling weak and confused. To suddenly lose control of all your bodily functions is difficult to accept. For Jeff, it was just one more thing to make him feel different. For me, it was something that I hoped would encourage him to gain control of his life.

More Tough Love

At the doctor's office, I sat in on Jeff's visits to help clarify when necessary. I also needed to get the doctor's input firsthand. Dr. Johnson had a direct manner, which I immediately liked. After a brief physical exam, the questions began. "What do you remember about your seizure, Jeff?" Dr. Johnson asked. "Not much at all," Jeff answered. The next question caught him off guard with its directness, "Are you drinking on a regular basis?" "Pretty much," was the answer. Dr. Johnson rose from behind his desk and faced Jeff directly. Gesturing with his hand, he continued, "Your normal brain was functioning here." He raised his hand to shoulder height. "Your head injury brought it to here." His hand dropped to his waist. "And now you're DRINKING and bringing it down to HERE!" The hand dropped lower. "Didn't anyone ever tell you that you shouldn't be drinking at all?" Jeff answered in a sheepish voice, "My mother." Dr. Johnson took a step forward and, placing his finger in Jeff's face, said forcefully, "YOU should have known better!" I wanted to jump up from my chair and applaud. This was tough love in action! I knew Dr. Johnson would be good for my son.

A New Challenge

Jeff was no longer working. Local buses didn't run during his night hours at the box factory. Also, being totally alone at his workplace was not wise at this time. Seizures are usually not life-threatening and generally stop after a few minutes. The danger lies in the possibility of striking the head in falling, or constricting the throat on something, such as the edge of a wastebasket. Another type of epilepsy produces multiple seizures. Unless quickly treated, these can be fatal. Thankfully, Jeff's first two seizures lasted only a few minutes. We weren't quite so lucky later on.

What Now?

Suddenly, Jeff was faced with another problem—boredom. No driving, no work, no place nearby to socialize, or as he would say, hang out. He had a work experience at a local supermarket, that lasted only four days and ended badly. Despite my efforts to explain his deficits, he was assigned bagging on a busy shopping day. That right hand simply couldn't keep up, and when a customer complained, Jeff responded with something unprintable, threw off his apron, and rushed home. He was livid. When I called to say he wouldn't be coming back; even if they wanted him, they were anything but understanding. I really couldn't blame them. They had no idea of his struggles.

State employment programs offered Jeff some help, but nothing met his needs, which were so difficult to perceive. One job suggested to him was that of a bouncer in a Newport nightclub. This 5'6" kid with a head injury—a bouncer?? At that point, we decided to conduct our own job search.

I returned to teaching in the fall of 1990. In an effort to provide some meaningful activity besides T.V. and his limited periods of reading, I had Jeff help me prepare my kindergarten classroom for the new school year. He still had his flair for art and could steady the ladder for his aging mom. I wouldn't let him climb it. Maplewood had referred to us as "the team" when we returned there for visits. It is essential that a head trauma victim have at least one person who understands and accepts him, unconditionally, just as he is. I thanked God daily that I could be that person. Together, we kept hope alive.

Pool to the Rescue

We moved frequently during the early years of the 90's. One of these moves brought us closer to my school and a billiards hall, which would greatly affect Jeff's life. It was called "Rack 'Em Up Billiards." Jeff was taken there by my friend's son, and it soon became his home away from home. The two brothers who owned the pool hall took Jeff under their wing. Jeff, in turn, did whatever he could to be helpful. At that time, no liquor was served there. For both Jeff and me, this was a monumental factor.

At the pool hall, he developed his pool skills, which was great exercise for his right arm. He also designed and constructed several sturdy benches for the brothers. It took him a few months, but they were state of the art when he finished. Equally important were the friendships that developed during these years. They supported him during failed job searches, periods of depression and the *grand mal* seizure that wouldn't stop.

This last could have ended tragically, but everyone did the right thing. His buddy eased him down as he fell, the owner called the paramedics, and two of the girls, when they couldn't reach me by phone, came and pounded on our apartment door to wake me up. May God bless them all!

When I reached the hospital that night, Jeff's body was still showing signs of tremors, but the Valium I.V. was beginning to control the seizures. There had been two at the pool hall and another as they arrived at the hospital. The human body can take only so much.

Just Another Challenge

In the past, when I reported a seizure to Dr. Johnson, he would ask, "Was there only one?" His response to my "Yes" was always "Good." I sensed that this was important to him; I was right. This last seizure had put Jeff in a different category. He had tests to see if his brain capacity had been diminished. His medications were reviewed and one was changed. It took Jeff about two weeks to regain his strength. He seemed to have lost interest in many things, including the pool hall. We talked, and he poured out of his thoughts and fears. What would they think of him? Would they even want him to come back?

I wondered myself if it was asking too much of Jeff's Rack 'Em Up friends to have him return. I called to discuss the pros ad cons. They readily welcomed him back and assured me that they would keep an eye on him. I was not to worry. I haven't seen these two good men for quite a few years, but I will always remember their kindness.

A Walk in the Rain

As Jeff neared his thirties, he began to spend less time at the pool hall. He was maturing, something doctors, early on, had not been sure he would do, considering the extent of his injury. He still had his periods of depression. The last episode that occurred at Rack 'Em Up, was on a rainy night. Jeff, as the owner described it, was standing against the wall. As he attempted to reach a chair, all the time talking incoherently, he stumbled and was steadied by a friend. He didn't know who or where he was. Paramedics were called, and then, I was called. The rain was pelting down as I arrived at the hospital. Jeff was conscious. He looked at me and said, "Don't hate me, Mom." I assured him that I could never hate him. He had been drinking. His tears came, as he said "Mom, I'm just a BIG NOTHING."

The hospital never called this a seizure, and noting his depressed state, hesitated to perform tests to determine if it had been. I assured them that I would call Dr. Johnson in the morning. It was 4:30 a.m. when Jeff was discharged. The rain was still coming down in torrents. We called twice for a cab, with no response, so we decided to walk the short distance home. It was spring and warm, even at this hour. The water in the streets was ankle deep. My umbrella was no help in the strong wind. Jeff and I linked arms. Strangely, as we looked around us, we had to laugh. What a sight we were! My spirits lifted. Things couldn't get worse; somehow, they would get better.

10

Where Do I Fit In?

Jeff's attempts to find work during the first fourteen years following his injury led him in many directions. Good-hearted people reached out to assist him. Frequently, the work was beyond his capabilities, either mentally or physically.

Memory was a serious problem. Often I would say to him, do THIS, and then do THAT. Jeff would return having done only THIS. He had no memory of the THAT. We finally were able to work together quite well, taking breaks when the job would begin to overwhelm him. We put together a number of prefab items. In time, he was doing more of the work than I, by following the directions, step by step, without the pressure of a time limit.

Early on, Jeff was admitted to Bristol Community College, despite his low math scores. He did well in a speech course, where he recited his favorite selections before the class. For the final, he wrote and delivered the story of his accident, which even impressed his classmates. He passed the course with a B+. The following semester, Jeff signed up for astronomy. He enjoyed using the telescopes to scan the night skies but could not retain the facts for written exams. He had to drop out. Obviously, college was not for him.

Doesn't He Care?

Supermarket managers, frame makers, vacuum salesmen, gas station owners, these and more, all interviewed this young man who couldn't work with numbers and couldn't remember multiple directions. They chose not to hire him, or in some instances, to not keep him on. These were not heartless businessmen, bent on making a profit. They simply didn't have the information necessary to deal with the "walking wounded."

Why doesn't he listen?
Why doesn't he work faster? I can't afford to hire him.
Why doesn't he control his frustrations?
Why doesn't he just try harder?
Doesn't he care?

Oh, yes, he cared—cared so much that his failure to find a job made him feel like a "big nothing." The morning after our pre-dawn trip through the flooded streets to our home, I called the school where I tutored. I told Mary, the secretary, that I wouldn't be in that day, that I needed to get some sleep and later take Jeff to his neurologist. Mary, being the concerned person she is, asked what had happened and assured me of prayers for my son.

As Jeff and I sat waiting to be picked up at the clinic that afternoon, I mentioned a forbidden subject—volunteer work. Jeff had previously vowed never to work without pay, refusing to see it as a therapy. I understood that he had never experienced the satisfaction of getting a good paycheck, but now, my main concern was his mental health. I feared the signs of serious depression he was exhibiting. Perhaps he could do some volunteer work at the small grammar school located behind our house, where I had taught for five years. He knew the staff well. I held my breath and waited for his answer. Jeff's reaction surprised and encouraged me. He thought this might be a good idea. I assured him that I would speak to the principal soon. I had retired a few years before, but still had close ties with what I continued to call my school.

A Helping Hand

Some will call what happened next simply a coincidence; I call it a God-incidence. The school was just dismissing when we arrived home, so I went over. Mary met me, looking concerned. She took me aside and said, "Mrs. Varley, I hope you don't mind that I shared what you told me this morning with the principal. We talked about it and thought Jeff might like to help the custodian two or three afternoons a week. We would like very much to have him here."

I was almost speechless! While Jeff and I had spoken of this possibility earlier, it was being discussed by Mary and the principal here at school. I suddenly felt the rush of "wind beneath my wings." Hope lived!

Jeff hadn't driven since his last *grand mal* seizure, the big one. More than six months had passed. I decided not to mention it. Perhaps setting up his new apartment was a healthy diversion.

The Right Move

We had recently moved into a tenement behind our church and school, where we each had a small apartment on the third floor. They were joined by what was called a fire door years ago. It enabled the tenants to escape through each other's apartments in case of fire. Fire escapes on the outside of the building were a later addition.

This move was a gift to Jeff and me. Since Jeff was only seventeen when injured, he had never known the responsibilities of independent living. Once seizures entered the picture, it was important that I be nearby to assist him. My obligation to prepare Jeff for life in the future weighed heavily upon me. I reminded him often, as I tried to share my motherly wisdom with him that I wasn't going to live forever. This apartment arrangement was the perfect answer. Our landlord, who was also our pastor, kindly adjusted the rent to make this move possible. May God bless him! Now Jeff was head of his own household. This new location placed us within easy walking distance of the school where Jeff had begun his volunteer custodial work, the pool hall where he still spent some of his evenings, and several convenient stores.

To Drive or Not to Drive

Two or three more months passed and there was still no mention of his driving. In his twenties, Jeff had lived to drive and complained mightily about the six-month restriction after a seizure. I couldn't contain my curiosity and asked him if he planned to contact Dr. Johnson for the usual medical O.K. His answer amazed me. He said that after giving it much thought, he had come to the conclusion that it would be safer on the road, for him and others, if he didn't drive again. Besides, it was just too expensive. I was truly proud of him. This was not an easy decision. Perhaps he would drive again at some point in the future, but at this moment, he had judged other things in life more important. My son was using good JUDGMENT! Alleluia!

The volunteer job at school was a positive thing in Jeff's life. The teachers praised him for his thoroughness, and he developed a friendly relationship with the custodian in charge. The only down side was the fact that he WAS a volunteer and had yet to find a paying job. With no money to take her out, how could he ever hope to have a relationship with a girl? To Jeff, this was no small matter. Later, this job would open the way to another, but that lay in the future.

Relationships

Head injured people often find it difficult to maintain a normal social life. It pained me to watch Jeff struggle with this. In our new neighborhood, he made friends with two young men living close by. They were cousins, each married, each with three children. Family was the center of their lives, and they included Jeff in many of their celebrations. When one needed help with a project, the other two were there to lend a hand; taking out tree roots; digging for a pool; then setting it up; and the list goes on. Their relationship continues to be a source of pleasure for Jeff. How grateful I am to all of them!

Girls were a different story. In his early teens, Jeff was chubby. The year before his accident, at seventeen, he slimmed down. His friend Karen became his girlfriend. Jeff was quietly delighted. Then came July 10, 1989 and the crash. His few female relationships since then had been short-lived, thankfully. They involved alcohol and an angry ex-boyfriend. As he reached his late twenties, with no job and his driving curtailed by seizures, Jeff felt that life was passing him by.

I tried to help him see his cup as half full by reminding him that he was still young, that there was a girl out there for him. His response was, "OH, yeah, Ma, well just WHERE is she?" As the years passed, Jeff became more low keyed about this subject, yet I sensed his pain; I knew it was the cause of his occasional drinking episodes. I have dreamed of that special woman who could live happily with my son. She would be able to look beyond his forgetfulness and lack of flexibility, beyond his jumps to judgment and flares of anger. She would need to see the heart. There she would find a sensitive, loving person, who puts effort into all he does, despite appearances. She would be his strength where there was weakness. God alone knows what path Jeff will take in this area in the future. It remains my hope and prayer that he will have relationships that enrich his life.

11

The Sun Rises

We never know what tomorrow will bring. How often I had said this to Jeff. In April of 2003, it proved to be true. Jeff, the volunteer, was about to become Jeff, the employee. One of the part-time secretaries at the school where he volunteered also worked part-time at a Catholic high school on the other side of the city. When a "Help Wanted" notice for a custodian was posted at the school, Denise thought of Jeff. She immediately went to the principal, whom she knew to be a kind, compassionate man. She told him about Jeff, the accident, and the good work he had done at her other school. Mr. McKeown did not disappoint her.

The following day, Denise announced the great news to me; the principal at St. Joseph's High School wanted to speak with Jeff about a job. He was to drop by for an application, fill it out and bring it to his interview. Jeff would drop by, but it would take two buses to get him there. At this time, neither of us drove. Giving up driving had been a difficult decision to make, until the idea of having Jeff learn the bus routes with me had come to mind. The timing couldn't have been better.

The Interview

One of the questions on the application was "In what way do you feel you can be a positive addition to our workplace?" We tossed around a few ideas. Then, Jeff wrote that he would work very hard, get along well with others, and be a good example to the students.

We rode the buses together on the day of the interview. After a quick lunch at Papa Gino's, I waited as Jeff walked away, application in hand. It was a long twenty minutes. He came back smiling. Mr. McKeown had said he would like to help Jeff. He was one of several candidates being considered and would hear from the school in a week or two. For years, I had been sure that somewhere in our city, there was an employer who would understand where Jeff was coming from, and still be willing to give him a chance. Hopefully, Mr. McKeown was that person.

Almost two weeks went by. Jeff said very little and I tried to stay upbeat. We went shopping early one morning and returned to find a message from Denise on Jeff's answering machine. Mr. McKeown would like to meet with him at 11:45 that day. Could he make it?

Jeff's answer was a resounding "yes." He was hopeful but felt that he would probably be told that his application had been filed for future reference. We reviewed the bus schedule for the number and time, and he was off. I looked out our third floor window as he walked toward the terminal. How often in the past, I had longed to say to him, "Good-bye, Son, have a good day at work." Perhaps that day was coming. Two hours went by, then a third and a fourth. I was on the verge of panic, when Jeff burst through the door. He was flushed, smiling, and wearing a red shirt with the white lettering: **St. Joseph School**, and under that: **Staff**. Jeff Varley had a job!

On arrival at the school, Mr. McKeown had asked him, "Do you still want to work here?" Jeff assured him that he did. "Then come with me," the principal said, "I'll get you a shirt and you can start right now." The following morning, as Jeff left for work, I said, "Good-bye, Jeff, have a good day." Tears of joy rolled down my face, as he closed the door. No doubt, there would be cloudy days, but that April morning, the sun had never been more brilliant.

49

A New Plan

Over the years, the several state work programs offered to Jeff lacked the necessary follow-through. Often, those involved, although well-informed themselves, did not seem to pass on sufficient knowledge to job placement groups regarding the specific needs of each client. It wasn't until the early 2000's that The Nine Trial Work Months Program was proposed. It set no limits to the hours one could work, be it part-time, full-time, or overtime. In this way, the person re-entering the work force was able to determine just how much he was able to do, both physically and emotionally.

The nine months were then followed by three more years of work. After each of these years, the worker was re-evaluated to determine his eligibility for continued benefits. At last, there was a program that Jeff could work with, one that offered support as needed.

Mr. McKeown felt it best that he begin by working four hours a day. Jeff was disappointed at first, but it didn't take long for him to realize the wisdom of this decision. He came home each day completely exhausted. Everyone is nervous beginning a new job, but for the head injured, there is the additional concern that he won't measure up, especially if his limitations are not visible. Jeff had the advantage of knowing that Mr. McKeown understood his past, but St. Joseph's was a big school.

His work for the first few weeks was on the first floor. Gradually, he got accustomed to the routine, but lack of speed, which will always be a problem for Jeff, was his big worry. He would come home and tell me that he didn't finish this or didn't do that. All I could advise him was to just do his best. A few weeks later he was transferred to the second floor. There were laboratories and other unfamiliar areas to clean. Jeff likes routine. Changes upset him, but, happily, after a few weeks, things eased up, and so did his anxiety. He was beginning to take things in stride and overcome some of his fears.

Getting in Sync

Jeff worked four hours a day for most of his nine trial work months. On occasion, especially during the summer, he would be asked to extend his hours when certain work needed to be completed. This gave him a chance to consider increasing his hours permanently. His physical strength had increased considerably since working. Yet, something Jeff couldn't quite understand held him back. He knew it wasn't laziness, and he certainly could use the money. Several months would pass before we would understand and discuss this matter.

At the completion of these trial work months. Jeff met with his social worker to go over phase two of the program, involving the next three years. In any given month, his gross income could not exceed a certain amount. Should it be over this total, he would not receive his social security benefits the following month. It would require close monitoring. This all seemed overwhelming to Jeff, but it would prove to be a good challenge for him.

Using calendar and calculators, we worked out just how much Jeff could make each month and still be under the total allowed. He was able to increase his hours to 4½ a day. Every day, he would record his hours worked and every month, make copies of his pay stubs to be sent to his caseworker. Jeff got up each work day two hours before leaving the house. He found this necessary in order to prepare his mind as well as his body for the hours ahead. This morning routine was very important to him, and he advised me not to interfere with it, if I expected a pleasant response. Being a cheerful person 24/7, I must admit I sometimes found this difficult.

The Gift

It was at this time that I began to understand why the injured brain responds as it does, under certain conditions. I had lived with the head injured Jeff for over fourteen years, but observing him in his new job gave me many more insights. Most of us wake up and go through multiple actions to prepare us for our day, but how much thought do we give to each of these actions, unless it's to select our breakfast cereal. We simply "go with the flow."

In Jeff's cerebral world, everything he did required concentrated thought. Life didn't flow, as it once did. He couldn't deal with more than one thing at a time. At work, this was often a source of anxiety, when schedule changes or the unexpected happened. How would he manage to do all that was expected? He usually managed well, with the help of his co-workers, who would simply advise him to calm down. Small wonder that after 4½ hours he was tired.

When Jeff and I finally did speak of these things, he seemed relieved. In difficult moments, I had always reminded him that, no, I couldn't get inside that head of his and know EXACTLY what he was feeling, but, of all the people in this world, I understood the best.

It had been my gift for as long as I could remember, this ability to experience within myself the feelings of others, sorrows as well as joys. Now, I could use this gift to help my son in his times of self-doubt and worry, and hear him say "Mom, that's JUST what I mean," or "That's EXACTLY what it's like."

There were also times when his words and actions didn't merit my approval. Then, I was just as quick to tell him that his behavior was not acceptable or not to be tolerated. And he knew I meant it!

12

Today

You may wonder, as you begin this final chapter, if it will conclude with the words, "And they lived happily ever after." No, it won't. For Jeff, and those much like him, there is no closure, no time when one can say, "Thank God, it's behind us! It's over! No more depression. No more drinking or drugs to ease he pain. No more deep concern about the future." But there is always hope. HOPE is the reason for writing Jeff's story. It is the only thing that sustains the walking wounded in our society and the loved ones who travel their journey in life with them, day after day. What follows are a few of the highs and lows encountered during the last three years.

Congratulations

"Mr. McKeown would like to see you in his office," was the message that greeted Jeff when he arrived at work in September 2004. His mind raced as he walked through the halls. What had he forgotten to do? It was the beginning of the new school year. Had someone complained? The office door was open. "Hi, Jeff," Mr. McKeown said from behind his desk. "Come on in, and sit down. Don't worry. Everything is fine." He then handed Jeff a letter from the River View Committee to Employ Persons With Disabilities. He further explained that St. Joseph's High School had chosen him to receive this award for "outstanding efforts and successful employment."

A banquet would be held at which Jeff, and eleven other people employed throughout the city, would be awarded a Certificate of Achievement by the mayor. The school had reserved a table for Jeff and seven of his relatives and friends. That afternoon, he handed me the letter informing him of this honor, like it was just a piece of ordinary mail and walked away. Later, he referred to it as "no big deal," but it was a huge deal. Jeff's smile, as he posed with the mayor a few weeks later, was the proof.

A Step Backwards

Despite the awards banquet and his own acknowledgment that he DID have the perfect job—for HIM, there were still periods of depression. A chance remark by a co-worker on a bad day, referring to their work as a dead-end job; a bus missed two days in a row, when others were zooming past him in their cars; a chance encounter with a girl that made him feel inadequate. Any one of these could have triggered the thought that a little pot would make him feel better.

I had no idea. Alcohol, yes, but not pot. Every night, Jeff went into his bedroom after work, closed the door and relaxed. Since we each had our own apartment, it was easy to keep me in the dark about HOW he was relaxing. I knew he was burning a lot of incense, but this had been his habit for a long time. My only clue was his behavior. It soon bordered on paranoid. People were watching him, and some were talking about him as he passed them on the street. He KNEW it! I called Dr. Johnson for advice. Only then, did Jeff admit that he was smoking pot each night—to feel better. My question to him was, "Well, DO you feel better?" "Mom, I can't stand the way I feel anymore!" It was as if he had seen for the first time where his actions were taking him, how close he had

54

Jeff with the Mayor, having just received an achievement award.

come to losing much of what he had worked so hard to accomplish.

It took two more days for Jeff to regain his mental balance. I was hopeful that what he had experienced was terrifying enough to keep him drug-free. So far, this appears to be the case.

Why?

Earlier in Jeff's recovery the officer who had called me from the police station, as Jeff sat drunk in a cell there, asked me the question, why? "Why is he doing this, after all he's been through? I see him riding his bike in town, and think how far he's come. Then, we find him like this. Why?"

Depression was the only answer I could give him. DEPRESSION is the monster that attacks so many of the walking wounded. It is difficult to judge the needs of those who look so normal. We expect them to measure up to certain standards. By doing so, we are not being unkind, just uninformed. Doors open and ramps are installed for the handicapped who come in wheelchairs, on crutches, blind, or missing limbs, and well there should be, but those whose handicap is hidden deep within the brain, are just as needy, sometimes more.

Twice Born Son

When I walked into Grayson Memorial Hospital eighteen years ago, I was among the uninformed. Only my brief working experience at a rehab center had given me a glimpse of what lay ahead. It was through the information shared along the way by Jeff's many kind caregivers that I came to understand this group of precious people, known in medical circles as "the walking wounded." Today, there are so many of them. Speed and the injuries of war have made head injuries almost epidemic.

As the years have passed, a well-meaning friend said to me, "You really haven't had a life since Jeff's accident, have you?" I don't remember just how I responded, but I began to think seriously about her words. True, my life had been profoundly impacted by Jeff's injury. Decisions were then made with an eye on how they would affect him. Would I go here? Could I do that? Sometimes one crisis seemed to follow on the heels of another, but never did I feel that I "haven't had a life" since then.

Today, I can write my response. No, it wasn't the life I had anticipated after Jeff's father and I parted. On July 10, 1989, I was asked to give my son life for a second time, to be there for him, unconditionally. He was now my twice born son, as dependent on me, at times, as he had been as a child. I was to nurture and instruct him, having as my goal, that of every mother, the raising of a son who is ready to face the world. Jeff will need help occasionally when I'm gone. He will have learned where to find it. Hopefully, it will be there.

I Believe in You

Several years ago, Jeff and I were visiting my grand niece, a young mother of three lovely girls. The conversation turned to Jeff's accident. We spent an hour sharing our story with Stacy. I told her of my hope to one day write a book that would be called *Twice Born Son.* When she rose to leave, Stacy said, "Auntie, you MUST write that book. It would be such a help to others."

The following Christmas, my gift from her was a packet of spiral notebooks and an encouraging card telling me to WRITE, that she believed in me. The seeds were sown, thanks to Stacy. Thank you, Honey! These notebooks, along with several paperbacks on head injury and how to cope with it, were placed on my bookcase in clear view. And there they sat. I continued to assure my friends that my book WOULD be written. It would be a kind of therapy for me, when the time was right. I did journal the events of Jeff's hospitalization at both Hope and Maplewood, but faced with the challenges of being home, writing the ups and down of each day was the last thing I wanted to do. At that time, the future had seemed very uncertain. Some days I felt ineffective and alone, as my hope was put to the test. I would write later.

Since childhood writing my thoughts had been my way of expressing joy and assuaging sorrow. I had written a few brief chapters in the early 2000's, but the turmoil of the times had sidetracked my efforts to continue. Friends encouraged me to write as a means of being able to leave Jeff a financial legacy, if my book proved successful. Still, I hesitated, wondering if it would generate enough interest. Perhaps, I thought, when Jeff reached a certain level of independence, I would be able to step back a bit, both physically and emotionally from his world. Then, I could view the years since his accident in the right perspective and produce a manuscript that reflected both truth and hope. It was in May of 2007 that I did take that step back and spent two weeks in South Carolina. There, each night as I watched the latest news of the escalating violence in Iraq, I found my answer. How many of our precious soldiers were being blown out of their vehicles and diagnosed with serious head injuries? OUR WALKING WOUNDED!

A Reason to Write

Now I could write, not just for Jeff and me, but for the many who are returning to our hospitals and later are reunited with their families, only to find that they are not the same people, not the same sons, daughters, husbands, wives, fathers, or mothers they were before their injury.

At the beginning of this book, I refer to Jeff's accident as "a mother's worst nightmare," and I still believe it is. I also said that I could never bear such a tragedy. Here, I was wrong. From the very depths of our being we are able to draw the strength to survive—and to HOPE. It is this hope that I desire to pass on to others—the mothers, fathers, and loved-ones of our wounded. There is truly no survival without it, no real quality of life for ourselves or the injured. In time, we accept that life will never be the same for anyone involved, but the new life that emerges can be filled with much that is beautiful and satisfying. Life takes on new values, and much that once annoyed us becomes of little consequence.

This is not to downplay the difficulties encountered on this journey. They are very real, but for every step backward, several steps forward follow. This ratio seems to increase in a positive manner, as years pass. I fight back tears whenever I hear reports of those who sustain head injuries. I think of the long road ahead of them and pray that they find the good care they deserve in excellent rehabilitation facilities, counseling for their families, and workplaces where they are welcomed with understanding.

Thank You, Son

Twice Born Son would not have been written without Jeff's cooperation and good will. As the book began to take shape, I realized that many things being recorded might be embarrassing to him. This I could never do. Simply asking didn't seem sufficient, so I chose to read him each chapter as it was written. On occasion, I inquired a second time and even a third, when the material was especially sensitive. Was it really O.K.? Each time his answer was, "It's fine, Mom. After all, it's exactly what happened." To my courageous son, I say, "Thank you! I love you!"

And to you, who have chosen to read this book, Jeff and I say, "Remember, Hope lives!"

"The Team"—Jeff and his Mom.